MW00808988

STRANGE VICTORY

Sara Teasdale

Strange Victory
Sara Teasdale

This paperback edition
Published 2016

ISBN: 978-1907119347
All rights reserved.

Publisher: Tigmor Books
www.tigmorbooks.co.uk

Contents

III

I

Moon's Ending

Moon, worn thin to the width of a quill,
In the dawn clouds flying,
How to go, light into light, and still
Giving light, dying.

Wisdom

Oh to relinquish, with no more of sound
Than the bent bough's when the bright apples
fall;
Oh to let go, without a cry or call
That can be heard by any above ground;
Let the dead know, but not the living see—
The dead who loved me will not suffer, knowing
It is all one, the coming or the going,
If I have kept the last, essential me.
If that is safe, then I am safe indeed,
It is my citadel, my church, my home,
My mother and my child, my constant friend;
It is my music, making for my need
A pæan like the cymbals of the foam,
Or silence, level, spacious without end.

Autumn on the Beaches

Not more blue at the dawn of the world,
Not more virgin or more gay,
Never in all the million years
Was the sea happier than today.

The sand was not more trackless then,
Morning more stainless or more cold—
Only the forest and the fields
Know that the year is old.

Advice to a Girl

No one worth possessing
Can be quite possessed;
Lay that on your heart,
My young angry dear;
This truth, this hard and precious stone,
Lay it on your hot cheek,
Let it hide your tear.
Hold it like a crystal
When you are alone
And gaze in the depths of the icy stone.
Long, look long and you will be blessed:
No one worth possessing
Can be quite possessed.

Age

Brooks sing in the spring
And in the summer cease;
I who sang in my youth
Now hold my peace;
Youth is a noisy stream
Chattering over the ground,
But the sad wisdom of age
Wells up without sound.

Even Today

What if the bridge men built goes down,
What if the torrent sweeps the town,
The hills are safe, the hills remain,
And hills are happy in the rain,
If I can climb the hills and find
A small square cottage to my mind,
A lonely but a cleanly house
With shelves too bare to tempt a mouse,
Whatever years remain to me
I shall live out in dignity.

Truce

Take heart, for now the battle is half over,
We have not shamed our sires;
Pride, the lone pennon, ravelled by the storm-
wind
Stands in the sunset fires.

It may be, with the coming-on of evening
We shall be granted unassailed repose,
And what is left of dusk will be less darkness
Then luminous air, on which the crescent glows.

II

Strange Victory

To this, to this, after my hope was lost,
To this strange victory;
To find you with the living, not the dead,
To find you glad of me;
To find you wounded even less than I,
Moving as I across the stricken plain;
After the battle to have found your voice
Lifted above the slain.

Secret Treasure

Fear not that my music seems
Like water locked in winter streams;
You are the sun that many a time
Thawed those rivers into rhyme,
But let them for a while remain
A hidden music in my brain.

Unmeaning phrase and wordless measure,
That unencumbered loveliness
Which is a poet's secret treasure
Sings in me now, and sings no less
That even for your lenient eyes
It will not live in written guise.

Last Prelude

If this shall be the last time
The melody flies upward
With its rush of sparks in flight,
Let me go up with it in fire and laughter,
Or let me drown if need be
Lost in the swirl of light.

The violins are turning, whimpering, catching
thunder
From the suppressed dark agony of viols—
Once more let heaven clutch me, plunge me under
Miles on uncounted miles.

In a Darkening Garden

Gather together, against the coming of night,
All that we played with here,
Toys and fruits, the quill from the sea-bird's
    flight,
The small flute, hollow and clear;
The apple that was not eaten, the grapes
    untasted—
Let them be put away.
They served for us, I would not have them
    wasted,
They lasted our day.

To M.

Till the last sleep, from the blind waking at birth,
Bearing the weight of the years between the two,
I shall find no better thing upon the earth
Than the wilful, noble, faulty thing which is you.

You have not failed me; but if you too should fail
    me,
Being human, bound on your own inviolate quest,
No matter now what the years do to assail me
I shall go, in some sort, a victor, down to my rest.

Ashes

Laid in a quiet corner of the world,
There will be left no more of me some night
Than the lone bat could carry in his flight
Over the meadows when the moon is furled;
I shall be then so little, and so lost,
Only the many-fingered rain will find me,
And i have taken thought to leave behind me
Nothing to feel the long on-coming frost.

Now without sorrow and without elation
I can lay down my body, nor deplore
How little, with her insufficient ration,
Life has to feed us—but these hands, must they
Go in the same blank, ignominious way,
And fold upon themselves, at last, no more?

In Memory of Vachel Lindsay

"Deep in the ages," you said, "deep in the ages,"
And, "To live in mankind is far more than to live
    in a name."
You are deep in the ages, now, deep in the ages,
You whom the world could not break, nor the
    years tame.

Fly out, fly on, eagle that is not forgotten,
Fly straight to the innermost light, you who loved
    sun in your eyes,
Free of the fret, free of the weight of living,
Bravest among the brave, gayest among the wise.

Grace Before Sleep

How can our minds and bodies be
Grateful enough that we have spent
Here in this generous room, we three,
This evening of content?
Each one of us has walked through storm
And fled the wolves along the road;
But here the hearth is wide and warm,
And for this shelter and this light
Accept, O Lord, our thanks tonight.

III

"All That Was Mortal"

All that was mortal shall be burned away,
All that was mind shall have been put to sleep,
Only the spirit shall awake to say
What the deep says to the deep;
But for an instant, for it too is fleeting—
As on a field with new snow everywhere,
Footprints of birds record a brief alighting
In flight begun and ended in the air.

To the Sea

Bitter and beautiful, sing no more;
Scarf of spindrift strewn on the shore,
Burn no more in the noon-day light,
Let there be night for me, let there be night.

On the restless beaches I used to range
The two that I loved have walked with me—
I saw them change and my own heart change—
I cannot face the unchanging sea.

Return to a Country House

Nothing but darkness enters in this room,
Nothing but darkness and the winter night,
Yet on this bed once years ago a light
Silvered the sheets with an unearthly bloom;
It was the planet Venus in the west
Casting a square of brightness on this bed,
And in that light your dark and lovely head
Lay for a while and seemed to be at rest.

But that light is gone, and that no more
Even if it were here, would you be here,—
That is one line in a long tragic play
That has been acted many times before,
And acted best when not a single tear
Falls,—when the mind and not the heart holds
sway.

"Since Death Brushed Past Me"

Since Death brushed past me once more today,
Let me say quickly what I must say:
Take without shame the love I give you,
Take it before I am hurried away.

You are intrepid, noble, kind,
My heart goes to you with my mind,
The plummet of your thought is long
Sunk in deep water, cold with song.
You are all I asked, my dear—
My words are said, my way is clear.

To a Child Watching the Gulls

(Queenstown Harbour)

The painted light was on their underwings,
And on their firm curved breasts the painted light;
Sailing they swerved in the red air of sunset
With petulant cries unworthy of their flight;
But on their underwings that fleeting splendor,
Those chilly breasts an instant burning red—
You who are young, O you who will outlive me,
Remember them for the indifferent dead.

Lines

These are the ultimate highlands,
Like chord on chord of music
Climbing to rest
On the highest peak and the bluest
Large on the luminous heavens
Deep in the west.

"There Will Be Rest"

There will be rest, and sure stars shining
Over the roof-tops crowned with snow,
A reign of rest, serene forgetting,
The music of stillness holy and low.

I will make this world of my devising
Out of a dream in my lonely mind,
I shall find the crystal of peace,—above me
Stars I shall find.

Made in the USA
Monee, IL
11 July 2020

36414217R00023